The Tree
of
Life

G.M. Silva Neto

About the Author

G.M. Silva Neto was born in 1979 in Brazil and at the age of 16 moved to Australia, where he attended St Paul's College, Manly, and was later awarded an International Merit (Foundation Program) Scholarship to study for a combined Bachelor of Arts and Law at the University of Sydney. He tutored philosophy at St John's College while developing a career as a writer, and continued studying literature at the University of Oxford (Jesus College), where he won the 2008–9 D.L. Chapman Memorial Prize for an Original Composition in English Verse or Prose, published in the Oxford Alumni Annual, and graduated from the Master of Studies in Creative Writing with a thesis analysing the concept of selfhood in the modern Bildungsroman. He is a novelist, an accredited professional translator and a member of the Royal Society of Literature.

Paperback English version ISBN 978-85-917249-1-8
(ePub bilingual edition English-Portuguese ISBN 978-85-917249-3-2)
(ePub English version ISBN 978-85-917249-0-1)
(Hardback English version ISBN 978-85-917249-2-5)
(Paperback bilingual edition English-Portuguese ISBN 978-85-917249-4-9)

Printed in the United States of America

The Tree of Life   7

Epigraph   9

Seed   10

Root   18

Trunk   22

Branches   50

Flower & Fruit   68

This poem is dedicated to my Bengala friends,
to Mauro C. Balieiro,
and to Marisa Giannecchini.

The Tree
of
Life

And what is life,
if not a journey toward ourselves?

Seed

I am everything
and I am nothing at all

All that already exists
but is yet to come

I am the nameless and the indefinable,
the reality in which infinity is within,
the structural substance of time

I am all there is
and all that will ever be,
the seven branches that grow outwards and inwards
from time-reality

I am the fundamental existence behind every phenomenon
the single connection between all forms of creation
the absolute creating principle underlying all things

I transcend and permeate all reality
while I am every reality,
I exist outside cause and effect, space and time
while I am cause and effect, space, and time

I am the direction of the progress of existence
the constant imminence of manifestation
the sound that cannot be heard

I am the beginning,
the middle,
and the end

I am the first creation,
the only event without a cause,
a seed of light from nothingness

I am the highest temperature
expansion and cooling
the birth of space-time continuum
light, travelling through darkness

I am vastness and emptiness
the darkness and the void
the infinite within the finite
potential, manifest and not manifest

I am chaos and order;
the chaos in the order and
the order in the chaos

I am self-division into atoms and forms,
the birth of particles of matter and anti-matter in the vacuum
within the immovable silence

I am mathematical principles yet to be discovered,
the concept of numbers yet to be imagined,
pi and the golden ratio

I am motion and rest,
nuclear forces, electromagnetism and gravity,
the eternal dance of stability with instability,
diversity generating unity,
energy becoming laws
in the long passage of time

I am swirls of luminous milky-blue dots around a bright centre,
dust clouds, hydrogen and helium
nitrogen, oxygen and carbon
pressure creating heat at a core triggering thermonuclear fusion
I am, at last,
a star

I am ignited rock, cooling
proximity and the right temperature
liquid water

I am the chance and coincidence within certitude

I am the necessary certainty of the universe

Root

I am Life,
difference,
and evolution

Air, fire, earth and water
sunrays hitting rocks, mountains, and the ocean
storms over desolate peaks
prisms of light in the deep blue sea

I am an organic molecule
a simple cell
bacteria performing photosynthesis
multicellular life

I am adaptation, survival and endurance
immanent instinct
the inherent struggle for survival in the heart of nature
reflected in the heart of all living things

I am life living on life

I am DNA copying itself almost perfectly,
the constant birth of the new

I am fish, terrestrial plant, insect, amphibian, reptile, bird, mammal,
before I am a 'thinking man'

I am a hunter and a gatherer
an explorer who sees frontiers everywhere,
the settler of a field

I am the spring in the heart of winter
and the invisible birth of autumn in the high summer

I am the natural realisation of destiny
along the passing of time

Trunk

I am love, lust and orgasm
a point of intersection between two lines

A seed of my father
in the soil of my mother

I am the first one to arrive,
the meeting and the miracle of the union of opposites

I am life within another life

A piece of the universe aware of itself

The cycle of creation giving birth to its own existence

I am my first heartbeat

I am awareness
and the birth of reality

I am gestation and expectation
the creation of an unbreakable bond
before I am separation
and the invisible umbilical cord that will always be present

I am animal and I am spirit
the expression of selfhood through molecules and atoms
a conscious surface above infinite unconscious depth

I am Atman, borrowed essence and breath,
energy shaping a body of liquified, recycled hydrogen and oxygen,
billions of years old, from other stars

Now I am the day and the night,
the moon and the sun

I am milk, animals and vegetables
earth and minerals
sunlight and rain
sparkling curious eyes

I am my mother and my father, and
I'm neither my mother nor my father

I am feeling and consciousness
hunger and thirst
skin, muscle, fat and bones
a heart that beats as an expression of a will to live

I am the movement of joints
circulation of blood, digestion
processing of information
tissue repair

I am touch, colours, sounds, tastes and smells
their unconnected meanings
trillions of cells and a mind which has no cells

I am the first word on the page
the first stroke of paint on a blank canvas
the infinite possibilities that exist in white
and in time to come

Infinite other lives permeate my life

I stand naked before the sun

I don't know that I know nothing,
while I have within me the entire knowledge of the universe

I do not yet understand,
but I already belong

I am my first step

I am play, toys,
bright primary colours,
my first smile

The free expression of truth from my innermost being

I am pencil-yellow sunshine
blue skies, green grass
a hilltop white house
with smoke curling up from its chimney

And I am also confusion and angst
thoughts and emotions
dreams and nightmares
hopes and fears
rainy days and leaden skies
long winters
a witness of arguments
the feeling of powerlessness
a wet bird in the nest during a thunderstorm

I am fear of the unknown
and fear of the dark

What I imagine is real,
and I am afraid of creatures of my imagination

I believe in everything I see, in everything I hear,
that adults have all the answers

I am pollen in the wind

I am the meaning of fairy tales
sunlight filtering through the trees
the first sight of the sea

I am my first puppy and shared frolic joy,
the new bike at Christmas
and the companion of the air on the first ride

I am moving legs, waving arms, dusty feet
scratched knees and bruised shins
the falling and crying
the getting up and laughing
fake tears and permanent scars

I'm small and I'm a giant
I'm cruel and I'm kind
I'm the naked raw truth,
the necessary and the unnecessary lies

I am the touch of a ladybird and
the insensibility of the head of a hammer,
the flight of a hawk and
the flapping of the wings of a butterfly

I am the one who follows the song of birds that sing within,
the one who climbs trees and chases
fireflies on a warm summer's evening

I am the one who wishes upon a star,
who takes lungfuls of the smell of wet earth as it starts to rain,
who raises his face to greet a sunray,
who breathes the Divine
and is in contact with the All without realising

I am a young shepherd in mythical Arcadia

I am words and the learning of other symbols
the connection of images, sounds and feelings to meaning,
inner states dictating the nature of thoughts
and shaping the reality around me

I am Achilles
and the soldier who is not Achilles

I am will,
the creation of personal destiny,
promise and infinite possibilities,
everything that I will be and
everything that I am not

I miss what I'm yet to become

I am knowledge of good and evil

I am my first kiss
lust and centred pleasure
Eros and Psyche
Apollo chasing Daphne
blood kindled by sheer desire

I am virginity and imagination before I am
skin contact, saliva, breath, sweat, rhythm and impulse,
arrows being released or opening flowers

I am surface life
the image on the bathroom mirror
the desire for proportion
awkwardness and lack of control

I see myself from the outside

I am existence looking outwards
but only seeing a reflection of what is within

I am an unbridled black horse defying authority

I know it all knowing nothing

I'm dust while I am the centre of the universe

I am what I think I am,
and I think I am Achilles

I am the search of who I am
and wonder where the final frontier is,
within and outside of me

I seek 'myself' and I seek 'the All'
without knowing that which I seek is me and
the All is also all around me

I am a tapestry of meanings
created in relation to myself and the outside world

I am unrelenting search for truth

I am my own theories, opinions and quotations
(which are mostly other people's)

I now know that I know nothing

I am the world of Ideas and Forms
the world of becoming and passing away;
I'm either Plato or Aristotle

I am a ship leaving port
the tip of a prow braving into an uncharted sea in the fog,
the first flight of a bird leaving the nest
to seek *eudaimonia* through flourishing *arete*

I am Ideals

And I can change the world

Branches

I am my friends

I'm there under cloud, rain and sunshine

I am companionship, trust and loyalty
the one who supports and the one who receives support,
myself inside another

I am the one who shares the sap from the same tree

I branch with and through other people,
every encounter a new leaf

I am my first day of work,
aspiration to leave footprints in rocks,
time marked by a watch,
tenacity between Monday morning
and Sunday afternoon sunshine

I am the one who believes in himself,
the one who gets up and begins each morning anew,
the one who carves the statue to the sound
of the best song he has within,
the one who fishes with good bait,
the one who opens a new way if he doesn't find one

I am the one who lays the bricks, who builds the roads,
who delivers the mail, who leads the nation,
the one who changes and moves the world forward

I am also a bank account,
a merchant banker and a Samaritan,
a handshake that hires and a pointing finger that fires,
no longer spirit, no longer human,
but part machine, part numbers, part profit
(Time is no longer time but money, toys have never existed,
songbirds are no longer expected on the clothes line)
but I am the one who closes the deal, who builds,
who also changes and moves the world forward

I am the one who has forgotten about the All
who breathes the smoky air of the city streets
who has the rhythm of the traffic lights
who no longer believes in everything he sees,
in everything he hears,
who knows that adults don't have all the answers,
who forgot that his destiny
is ultimately tied to the destiny of everyone

I am hopes and dreams
id, ego and superego
the individuation of everything I am

I am free will
while I'm bound by my personality

I'm shades of grey, shades of meaning, shades of myself,
the common soldier wishing to be Achilles

I am relentless striving for self-knowledge and self-improvement
the aiming of excellence
lead purifying itself to become gold
Ulysses tied up to the mast while the sirens sing

I am high ambition and the necessary instinct of self-survival,
the indefatigable determination of a young immigrant
pursuing a dream

I am David against Goliath

I am also compassion and indifference
faith and despair
war and peace
resoluteness and hesitation
courage and fear
pride and humbleness
audacity and timidity
gladness and regret
union and dissolution
trial and learning
error and flawlessness

I am my best friend and my worst enemy
sleepless nights and daydreams
a bowman not knowing he is the target
a hunter not knowing he is the prey

I am sun and rain
black and white
asphalt and dirt track
logic and the illogical
metal and air

I am somebody and I'm a nobody,
I matter and I don't matter

I am the Spartan who wears the crimson cloak and defends the pass,
regardless of the odds

I'm the one in the line of fire
who does not leave anyone behind
before I am a Purple Heart

I am the soldier who fights for peace before a war

I am the solitary traveller crossing the distant mountain range

I'm the house whose windows are turned to the West,
the faraway island within which only I will ever live

I'm the one who no longer believes he can change the world,
that the Realm of the Divine is outside and far from himself,
the one who now sees Ideals as just ideals
the one who realises that the world is empty of meaning
except for the one he gives

I am sincere prayer for a better life

I am one more in six billion
in an isolated planet spinning in the void
in one of the four hundred billion stars of a galaxy
amongst trillions and trillions of galaxies

I am the one in winter crossing the valley of ashes

I am the light contained in the presence of hope

I am part of somebody I long to find
a dandelion floating in possibilities
through city, field and wood
until I am, at last,
the meeting with a soil
in which to take root

I am a hand gathering flowers,
the one who bows and takes his sandals off
before entering the inner sanctum

I am the sense of certainty that destiny really exists,
the house whose windows open to the East
and sees the destined one as the sun

I am love that loves me back
colours regaining their colour from grey

I am the wish that a moment could last years,
the desire of being better than I was, than I am, than I will be

I am clasped hands and the adjustment of the stride
the silhouette of two intertwined trees
growing in the colours of the sunrise

I am the one who listens to the pulse of another heart
and realises it's his own,
the one who sees love
reflected in the actions and in the eyes of another

I am the sharing of most sincere aspirations
the telling and listening of deepest and darkest secrets,
complete trust and devotion

I am no longer one

but two

Flower &
Fruit

I am the vows
the lovemaking, the commitment
the routine, the arguments and the amends
the friendship turned into companionship
the finding of my own pace within the adjusted stride

I am the days that are dots
that one by one become a line
which then intersects forming a new point

I am gestation,
a boy or a girl

I am the first time I hold another existence of myself in my arms,
the meaning of unconditional love

I am nappies, milk, joy, infinite care, plans
the one who loves so much he suffers, gladly
the one who now lives also for another

I am a mother and a father
while still being a son and a daughter

I am the one who sees himself in a version of himself

I am no longer two but three, four...

Through the one who came from me
I become once again a child
and thus re-enter the Kingdom

I am one more witness of a flourishing,
the one who cherishes the future of another,
the one who explains, who guides, who is a Truth

I am Santa Claus and the Tooth Fairy,
before I'm neither

I am the one who watches the first flight of a bird leaving the nest
to seek what I also sought

I am the presence in the absence
the weight of emptiness
stillness filled with vibrancy by memories
silence which is full of sound

I am no longer four or three, but two again

I am years that pass by in seconds,
the one who sees a seed of himself generate another seed

I am the one who senses the weight and the lightness
of the approaching twilight

I am all the people, situations, selves, ideas, books
that I've lived with and through

I am the words I said and the words I didn't say
what I did and what I failed to do
everything I remember and everything I forgot
the dreams I realised and the dreams I could not realise

I am what I should have been and was,
what I may have been but never was

I am how much I was able to let go
to let in the new

I am the constant flow of the river, of the waves of the sea,
unborn and undying

I'm not only life
but life passing through myself,
life passing through Life itself

I am truth within the Truth

I am my contribution,
a product of my time as much as a product of my soul

I am my own theories, opinions and quotations
(which are and aren't mostly mine)

I see myself from the inside

I am existence looking outwards
and seeing the other

I am compassion and the life within

I have become my brother's keeper
and all are my brothers

I know all things because I know myself

I believe the realm of the Divine is within me and outside of me

I'm no longer time marked by the clock
as I've felt the pulse of the progress of existence
and realised that clocks are not marking time,
but their own movement

I remember that everything
has always been and will always be connected

I feel the presence of the All
in a wheat field
in an empty chapel
in a drop of dew
in a seashell
in everything

Everything has become relative
and absolute at the same time

I no longer search for the final frontier
because I know there are no final frontiers,
within or outside me

I am my offspring and
I am not my offspring

I am what I leave behind,
and what I will not leave behind

I am still my past as much I already am my future

I am all my ancestors since the first beginning
the incalculable number of events
so that I could exist, now

I am memories forgotten,
memories that never existed
psychological truths that were never true
a product of my own creation

I am the one who realised that life outside changes
when life inside changes,
the one who then prayed in silence to himself

I am what I sowed and what I did not sow;
infinite other lives still permeate my life
and my life permeates infinite others

I've been the multitude of selves of my soul,
a multitude of selves that weren't in my soul,
and I am still myself

I have changed the world just because I lived

I was Achilles because I was myself,
because I loved much

I no longer fear the dark or the unknown,
what I imagine is and isn't real

I've learned to listen to silence and speak through it

I was able to listen, to sing, and to dance
to the tune of the invisible piper,
to the rhythm of my own music

I am the one who sang the song he was born to sing

I am the one who has returned victorious

I am still pollen in the wind

I still stand naked before the sun

I have seen it all:
the eternal cyclical movement of history, of life, of death
the creation of this and infinite other universes,
the materialisation of the same archetypes, of the same forms
dying and being reborn in a thousand different ways,
in a thousand different years...
I have seen it all, and yet, I have seen very little of everything

I will carry nothing with me
and yet, I will carry everything with me

I will take only what is within me
how much I loved
what I shared
whom I truly was

I no longer believe in the division between matter and spirit
but that matter is spirit manifest

I realise that Atman is Brahman
that the All is Love and Light
that above me and below me there are only stars and galaxies
only life brimming throughout the cosmos
and expressing itself in infinite forms

I reached the All through my heart
and realised that my soul
has always been the soul of everything and everyone else,
that my essence is that of the cosmos,
that love is truth

I made the two into one,
the inner like the outer,
the lower like the upper

I am the sacred marriage of the sun and the moon,
the fusion of opposites to become one,
gold after the long transmutation of lead

I've become a seed planted in good soil
which produced a good crop,
I've found the treasure in the field and
sold everything to keep the one good pearl

I have sought and found,
knocked, and was let in

I am no longer the day and the night:
I have become a passer-by

I'm no longer aspiration to leave footprints in rocks
but the trail that the flight of a bird leaves in the air,
that a gliding seagull leaves on the water,
that the sun leaves in the day

I am hopeful again for mankind

I am the one who looks back
and enjoys his life for a second time

I go in peace
for although I lived for myself,
I lived for something greater than myself,
for the benefit of all

I will return to be what ripens the fruit, what beats a heart,
the knowledge contained in a seed to grow toward the sun

I am no longer the wisdom of words, of ideas, of thoughts,
but wisdom which cannot be expressed by them

I am the one who felt the existence of ultimate reality,
the indivisible unity behind the apparent plethora of its expressions,
the one who saw the wake of light behind all things
as the very imprint of the All

I am the one who will miss his outward self,
the persona that has a name,
flawed and perfect, which will not exist again

I will miss Planet Earth

I am the now which is future and past
and the now which is just the now

I am just one more
while I am the only one
while I am everyone

I am the self which is also everything,
every self that ever was and will ever be:
a stone, a piece of wood, an x and a y
have already been me and they will be me

I've been a thousand lifetimes
and could be a thousand more if I wish

I'm not going to infinity
as I already am in infinity

I no longer fear death
as I realise I cannot truly die

All I am is what I truly loved

A finite life within an infinite existence

And I realise that since the beginning, even before I left,
I already was, inevitably,
going home

I am my last heartbeat

I am no longer consciousness of reality
but reality itself

And I will live for ever

For I am the first and the last
All that is seen and all that is unseen
All that has come, and all that will come to pass

I am the pilgrim and the destination
the seeker and the found

I am Alpha and Omega
Tao
OM
the Nirvana of a Buddha
the Three that is One
the Kingdom within
and the Kingdom that is spread upon the earth

I am birth, life and death

Expansion toward infinity until the end,
when I am
a new beginning

I am the root
the trunk
the branches
the flower
the fruit and the seed
of the eternal Tree of Life

*

www.gmsilvaneto.com
twitter @gmsilvaneto

www.ingramcontent.com/pod-product-compliance
Lightning Source LLC
Chambersburg PA
CBHW021934040426
42448CB00008B/1068